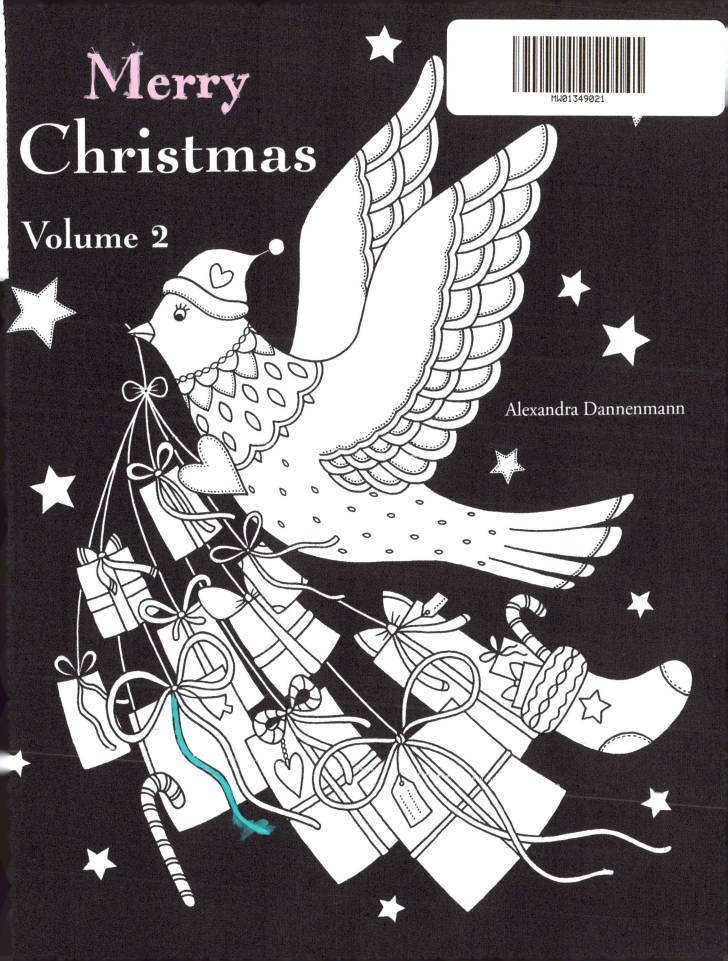

1st edition: October 2018
Copyright © 2018 Alexandra Dannenmann
Text and illustrations: Alexandra Dannenmann – Stuttgart
Translation: S. T. Paterson
www.facebook.com/alexandra.dannenmann
www.alexandra-dannenmann.de
All rights reserved.
ISBN: 978-1728815961

More colouring books by Alexandra Dannenmann:

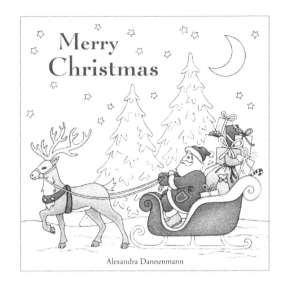
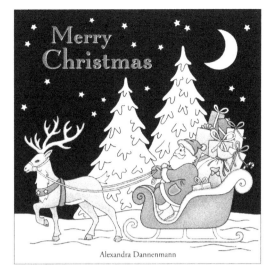

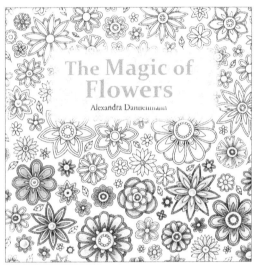
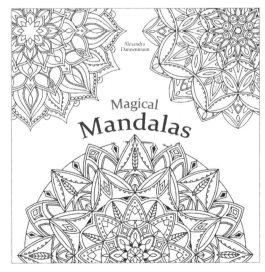

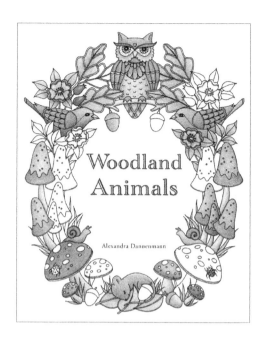

Find more information on my homepage http://alexandra-dannenmann.de or Facebook page http://www.facebook.com/alexandra.dannenmann.